Creature, Creature

CREATURE, CREATURE

To Phyllis & Don —
I hope you'll enjoy these
creepy, crawly midwestern
poems. All best wishes,
Rebecca
7-08-07
minneapolis

POEMS BY REBECCA ARONSON

Rebecca Aronson

MAIN-TRAVELED ROADS PRESS
Lewiston, Idaho

Main-Traveled Roads Press is a subsidiary of Sandhills Press, a small press devoted to the publication of Plains poetry for nearly thirty years. Main-Traveled Roads sponsors an annual poetry contest. *Creature, Creature* is the first recipient of the annual award.

ISBN: 0-911015-86-8
978-0-911015-86-7

Cover art by Dana Drum
Copyright © 2007 Dana Drum
danadrumart@yahoo.com

Table of Contents

Acknowledgments

Thanks to the editors of the following publications where these poems first appeared, sometimes in earlier versions:

The Alembic: "West"
Cimarron Review: "Love Poem," "Mosquito Mother"
Cranky Magazine: "Hopscotch"
The Cream City Review: "Aperture"
Ecotone: "Flash of Blue Catches in a Corner of the Hippocampus"
The Georgia Review: "Missouri," "Blacktop," "What Isn't There"
Gulf Stream: "Nocturne"
Kalliope: "Breeding Season" (Now titled "Mosquito Mother")
The Midwest Quarterly: "Subterranean"
The North Stone Review: "4am, Sitting in the Dark," "Beautiful Covers"
        (Now titled "Peonies")
Mare Nostrum: "Aerial"
Phoebe: "Fourteen Little Apologies" (Now titled "News of the World")
Prairie Lands Writing Project: "Grove"
Puerto del Sol: "Stitch"
Quarterly West: "Letter to John Berryman," "Kansas City Man Guilty of
        Five Murders"
RE:AL: "Conveyance," "Following You Up the Treehorn Trail"
Rio Grand Review: "Saint Theresa at the Apocalypse"
The Seattle Review: "In the Field"
Tin House: "The Question of Fire," "Handgun"

"Love Poem" was reprinted on the Verse Daily website (http://www.versedaily.
com) on Sunday, January 9th, 2005.

Thanks also to the many people whose suggestions and support have helped me shape this book: Linda Bierds, Richard Kenney, Colleen McElroy, Heather McHugh; my wonderful traveling writing group: Patricia Machmiller, Emmy Pérez, Oody Petty, and Renata Trietel; James Arthur, Joe Hafferbecker, Rebecca Hoogs, Johnny Horton, Jonathan Shapiro, Nancy Mayer, John Gallaher, William Walters, my parents Donald and Claire Aronson; and always Tim. Thanks to Dana Drum for her beautiful artwork. Special thanks also to Claire Davis for selecting it and to Mark Sanders for publishing it.

For Tim

You learn from animals. You learn in the dark.

-John Berryman, "The Animal Trainer"

I.

Missouri

Near Saint Joseph the fields sigh and corn stands up
against nearly any weather. Our sleep is filled
with still air in which thousands of crickets
ceaselessly rub their bandied legs
while we kick free of our blankets
in the night. It is a relief to hear you breathe,
your low snore a solid presence I recognize—
not quite my lost southwestern foothills
whose hunched silhouettes seemed so much protection,
but, still, something raised against the seamless prairie.
The sun comes in early, dragging the day's heat
in a close wake. We rattle among the bars of light
that stripe our rooms. Did you notice?
There are shadows from nothing but ourselves
where we walk in the ragged crab grass.

Blacktop

A girl leaps on cracked asphalt,
the hollow ball echoing its damp kisses
off all the doors as if the cars had been left
for acoustic purposes. And the light
is nearly done, so she's just a shining shadow—
reflective shoe stripes and the flaring edges
of loose sleeves. Her arms whir
and flash and her legs are floating glow-sticks
that disappear at the ends into dark socks
and dark shorts. The ball swooshes up
into invisibility and down to echo
where the ground spills wider
and already has swallowed the ringing pole.
The net is drawn to the streetlight's beam:
undrawn and drawn, a chain-link lung.

Aerial

In the church
an abandoned nest:
shallow bowl
of light, of stick and leaf
and lost feathers
spun in rubble.

Gravestone tiles
stain the floor
with a pattern
of portals.
From a bird's eye,
the highest pillar, the scene
is still
before the drop

down, drowning
in a doorway, down
to what resides
unseen, growing
another life.

A dust veil
on a girl. She reaches
into a brown bag,
withdraws a peach
that she holds to her nose
but does not eat.

Reliquary

The clavicle bell has a golden chime.
It rings my eye
up to a heaven of bone: see
the body's everlasting graces.
It makes a bridge, the spine, the small
ridges of the back
like stepping stones.

There are girls in the grotto,
mostly scattered. That one's complete
and Sunday-skirted,
the sticks of her fingers barely detectable
under her heavy rings
and lace, her wax face hides

a martyr's skull,
that cracked bud vase
tucked under her pillow
like a tooth.

I am wearing out my good body
today like every day.

As a child I drew face after face,
eye leading to nose,
nose to mouth, curve of chin
to loosed lock
of neighbor's hair, curl of cheek-
bone wisping into another's ear.
Everyone was part of someone else.

Here one man's femur

is the spine of a seraph's wing.
It swoops with terrible intention
from one dark corner toward the mariachi

propped opposite
in a skeletal chair
with a real guitar.

The floor is dirt
packed so hard
it's hard
to imagine
any worm ever
needled in.

Outside, a man
drops a wrapper
where he sits eating a sandwich
on a shaded bench
and a quick breeze
takes it away, the plastic

is almost nothing and he doesn't notice.
I think it will soon be

the wind chime in a bird's nest,
a casing remade,
a little rattle.

Navel & Blood

At Pearl Street the vendor is clutching handfuls of oranges,
armloads, unloading their sharp scent, their calendar of tricks.

With a quick knife to the navel each child gets a free section, a view
of the center, its spit in the eye and bitter mantle. One says,

it's like an armadillo, if they were sweet inside.

*

In full, our bodies, flush with multi-celled spheres,
our growth, globular, not just breasts, but elbows

and nostrils. Larynx. Cadmium globe after globe
aglow from such a good stirring, we are

blue under the zinc skin, chalk and cola—
an unerring exaltation, a lark of loose balloons...

*

Why dwell on the bite that bitters?

*

The vendor picks one from the middle as if by chance
to prove *all* their guts are good. At home each opened peel

reveals only a tight ball of dried-out string.

*

Every body is a den of dens.
Each thin wall contains its own warren
as when a mirror is held to a mirror.
We cluster and recur, rise like sugared yeast,

ingest and dispel ourselves. We season
and burnish, grow blowsy as apple blossoms.

*

In the January post a box of tangelo
and clementine, navel and blood.

A fingernail into pith sets summer smells loose.
Lemon-sucking sailors
we are, Midwesterners staving off winter.

We build a pyramid on the kitchen table,
this grove we are growing
of luminous refuse,
peels rising from the red Formica.

What Isn't There

Step inside, blind. A slow curtain
lifts here and there so that the black expanse

becomes a doorway and the eye finds
a chapel, finally, sweeping up

into a small dome, the painted-on sky a surprise. Cobalt.
It's not just about churches—

outside a woman sits in shadow, her palm
a ladle of sunlight to catch

a coin. Where her eye was is a small cave,
darkness closed with an unseen pucker.

Wanting a Child

After Jorie Graham

This morning I pick the stems of the parsley plant
clean of yellowed leaves. I sit on the porch swing
turning book pages until the swaying
makes me woozy. I drive
the cat off her perch and fill the washing machine
with hairy sheets. I watch as the sky turns white—
an inverted nest lined with tender feathers.
A crisscross of wires lingers into a distance
and disappears. The next block, the ocean, I couldn't say
where any one ends. My eyes catch at the hub
of lines, each leading to a horizon,
each riding quickly out of range.

Mosquito Mother

Egg sacs need to be filled. Built up.
Siphon what you can, girl, the babies are waiting.
Evening's hazy half-light shields you there,
sidling along screens, idle at the small rips
where a beetle snagged or rust
wore wire down to an entrance. Nearly invisible
even this close—a remote motor whining
its descent. Needle into the blue well.
After you've left, knowing nothing of the welt
where your thin straw went in. The fever.
Just this: one hot drop, tar in the belly,
that empty cavity now pulled drum tight.
Wing back slow and steady.

After Surgery

The up-running mice have gone, long time
since the pendulum quit its one-trick song.

Flowers someone left dimple and wilt, shred themselves
each day like penitents. The brain

rings its shop bells when thoughts step through.
They are mostly browsing. I'm fine

as china, as powder, as the line
between lethal heat and the heat that heals.

Circulation is a skill any body could master,
I'm just not a natural.

The clock says, *Disarm, disarm.*
No big deal—a pain pill grinds along

blocking any road it crosses. Nowhere to go,
but I think how quickly I'll get there.

Pepper

The body cannot digest black pepper.
—overheard

Small specks at sea, circulating the system,
arriving by river, moving in streams
from organ to island, walled in and swept along
by turns. We are all unsuitable particles
bound to a most unreasonable
despot, though she's barely aware
of her legions (amassing restless camps,
erecting ballasts against insignificance).
We're seasoned and salty as sailors
stationed for years in a weatherless ocean.
Reveille remains inconstant, faint alarms
rising from a distant hillock;
sometimes we drill, more often we drift
aimless and unmoored, on guard for jetsam
or dangerous roughage sent to flush us.

Subterranean

Gardens grow under fallen walls,
under cut stone and brim stone, deep down

under footfall, your heaviest tread
hardly resounds. Roots are moving

in all directions, sky eclipsed by earth so clouds
are soil and sun is soil and rain seeped down congeals

in soil. Gardens are buried under crumbled porticoes, grottos
grown hairy with fern, feelers of laurel, roses

upended, twisting into love knots. The bones of the buried
crosshatch, catch splinters of benches, fragments

of cup, teeth like charms from the dead.
Doorways rise to meet you, knocking at sidewalks, bleeding

into moss. What trips you is an arbor or an aphid,
cow's blood as it blossoms, after rain, into footprints.

The Way to Vanish

We are restless and leave our beds to cool.
Rain, but streets so hot they steam,
sidewalks slick with mud where dust was.

Where we walk a trench grows.
Old friends tumble in,
swim in the murk, flipping delicate feet.
The rain must blind me some.

Orange mushrooms glow
viperous on the lawns. They frighten me.
The lawns, too, frighten me. Mosquitoes
swim from their beds

multiplying as the rain does. A seed
of magnificence:
I expect to split in two,
split again and again
and disperse in the privet hedge.

Etruscan Love Song

There is no pet like a wing-footed lion, my treasure, my dove. Feed it olives, feed it broccoli, soothe its wiry locks. It's your spirit guard. It paces the kitchen, claw-clicks keeping time with a flute.

Mine is the monster, chained at the neck and grinning, a short stretch taut between claw and cobbler's demise. I surprise myself sometimes: temper, temper. But you're a star fruit, my duck, my feather. You're vision's best reach; I come down like weather. Or this: a pair of snakes, their winding and twining—I'm the tight embrace. Ask the goose of urns, soothsaying bird, to tell us what's to be: it only flaps, it lacks a voice, it lacks a place beyond the platter, the pluck and slaughter. Eat, eat, my grape; gnaw the wing that tells your fate.

Aperture

What the eye does: follows water's drop
from stone lip to the pause

behind the dancer's knee,
juts the long vee of street to the green

flare glimpsed at the far side
of a fountain's frame. I followed you there

to a courtyard where a yolk of light dripped thickly
through the leaves,

where a shadow's flicker revealed a hand
reaching to retract a shutter—

and then the heavy door yawned
to take you in.

Inside, beyond the pulpit's crown
dusty curtains sway. A cat stalks wind

in the entryway.

News of the World

I'm sorry. There are birds in the eaves. They swoop at the windows like suicides, and pull up sharp—*wait*—they become fingers that fidget in the walls.

I'm sorry. Everything is laid bare now that the leaves are off. The tree reveals its knotty hold, its crown of findings; at the root, canopies of bared ferns, sheltering fronds fallen away: secret of rabbits, of feral cats. We are open to the world and do not know it. What use the nightly news? A glass of water could tell you as much. Or the garden's deadest plant. Before the winter, autumn stalled and stalled. The severe rake, then sleep.

I'm sorry. The earthworms are dying on the floor. What's not to regret in storm drains, in plastic baskets where clean clothes gather particles? Such waste. Washing things away, when outside the sky is the most perfect, clotted blue.

The Question of Fire

Because it pours color in its path.
Because all things in it come down to the bones of bones, particles
more elemental than dirt.
Because its roar reminds us of nothing.
Imagine a basket of flame: always emptying, always full.
Because it was begun from one word (tree) held too close
to another (lightning).
Because of embers, those handfuls of history, and the potential of matches—
a future that any careless carrying might ignite.
Because there is no net, no cure, no promise.
Because we have been captured.

Rapture: the first curl of smoke quickening into blue and how it grows up
the way a kiss surprises (only lips on lips yet
the body suffused with ticking)
so that suddenly it's a real engine-red.

The fingers of grass along the alley know it
but lean in anyway and are consumed.
Because it calls to be fed and feeding will never surfeit.
Because to live is to hunger and nothing is more alien
and more familiar than the hunger of another.

II.

Spectacle

Beads of early apples reddening on slim branches
    (will they break? when the apples
are grown?). Each one I pick or pick up
has been tasted, a hole bored in,
one sated worm, or more.
        There are circles in everything. Trunk built of rings,
little O of insect burrow, disks of sun tunneled down
from leaf to limb, eye in its socket, a jay
watching me watch it...
        The eye's habit is motion always, flash, flash:
reaching for a shadow, a cup set down
where there is no table. The log at the back of the yard
that suddenly shifts at sundown
as a sleeper stirring, as a crouched predator switching
the tip of its tail in the weeds.
        (All afternoon under cover of the overgrown—
clashes.)
        Or this: a hill I used to go to
from which I'd see mysterious movers:
low reddish lights in continual motion,
one after another across the nighttime sky.
Some nights nothing at all.
        Daylight brought no insight, no nearby airport,
no pattern pressed or scorched into the grass. But what to look for?
Did I see and not know I saw?
        On a night walk through the house (the cat
two glowing spheres or a dark scrap
where foot meets fur briefly in mid-step) I trip
on invisible chairs and must close my eyes
to navigate.

Grove

A hundred orange poppies with their crepe-paper wings.
Seed heads full of syrup and germ.

Someone once stayed
who all winter thought about death.

Evidence: the overgrown, un-groomed apple tree blooms first.
When the apple blossoms shrivel and blow away,
the tulips.
When the tulips lose their sleek shells,
a sash of tiny daisies spreads across the yard.

Forsythia. Viburnum. Fiddleheads unrolling...

I know just where Kansas is from here. (We went last weekend
in our green car. We parked on the street in Lawrence.
No stockinged legs protruding from the undercarriage,
though there was a small dog
yelping on its string leash.
None of us expressed a wish for anything.)

The sun is in the garden
making lanterns of the petals.

Storm-seeds sow funnels
in the leaves.

Kansas City Man Guilty of Five Murders

Earth takes everything: leaf fall and fallen feathers,
takes lost nickels, single strands of hair and unbodied sweaters.
Swallows it up in a casket altogether. No matter
how a thing went down earth ingests it
just the same. I like to keep things separate,
with edges. Five is a sharp number, deceivingly
round, but get your hands around it
and it'll prick. Five. The number of bodies
that fit into a fifty-five gallon barrel.
See, a kind of joke: a barrel just like a number—
smooth in a way, but try to lift it, hold yourself close,
and the slats are hard as a skate blade.
Numbers are magnets, pull things in.
Each to its place is called, my mother'd say.
Is this mine? Five terms, my life five times,
the sum of fifty-five is more than five and five. Sounds odd,
but feels even. Feels like the smooth edge of a girl's skate,
the perfect shine, held tight to the chest, tighter,
until the cold metal cuts through.

Handgun

The muzzle in the hand, smooth and cool
the way the family dog's was.
That sweet pup. Always at the ready.
There was a rope we sometimes tied her to.
Fraying. Her pacing and pacing

around the wrought iron railing till the cord wore down
and she'd take off running awhile.
Always came back. What was inside her,
keeping her steady, must've been just like that.
Something wearing until she wasn't bound to us anymore,
and she broke. Bit a neighbor, then the baby.

No more time to bide. Too late
to come back. Left us nothing to rely on—
just this beauty: smooth and steady.

Diary of Light

If you bend to the water's face you'll see the galleries beyond the shutters. Three fat koi swim from the windows. There's a chair in the corner. The shadow of a wall hung with frames. Light in light equals an entrance. Can we not go in? A mirror, then, is more than an echo, as with the game I used to play: holding a looking glass in front to move by reflection. The whole world charged with angles, suddenly there were openings everywhere. In the pond everything strives for the surface: a fish at your shoulder, doorway to fish, fisheye, fisheye, your lips a kissing carp.

*

Mouth to mouth at the bathroom mirror I fog my own face into oblivion. How to know how you look? Lean in. Turn quick. Once on returning from a party I sat on the sink to watch my pupils dilate and shrink as I moved close and away from the light. The eye itself a little glass: the bulb a bright glint, and there I am: inside. Apple of my own eye. Girl in a dark orb. Gesturing.

*

The cat asleep pressed to the snake tank and the snake asleep on its heated rock, its head inches from the glass wall and the cat's face. I switch on the light. Four open eyes. Two bodies in rapid retreat. A cartoon. Or again to the cat, who sometimes looks behind the mirror that leans against the bedroom wall. She's never there. But who *doesn't* wish to step through? Reach out as if starting an embrace, hand outstretched toward heart. Enter through your own shirt. Try to be your best self.

West

Across the road a yellow Bobcat
    chews a ragged border of mud along the field.
        My boot treads slick against asphalt,
    I slide too near a speeding hotrod—farm boys
in a patch-job coupe shaking off a day of steering slow tractors
    in straight lines, reddened arms loose in the windows, a beer
        already cradled between stiff-jeaned knees.
    I only imagine these boys.

Is Spring this symphony of mowers
    roaring in overlap, overriding the robins
        perched everywhere in the damp grass
    masticating like tiny cows?

After rain there are earthworms
    wriggling on the sunroom floor. They must tunnel in
        at the borders. My husband warns me, *we've got worms, honey,*
    and I laugh until I see them, maybe thirty,
wet bodies glistening as they shimmy
    from the corners. Even the cat, momentarily fascinated,
        soon puts her ears back and tiptoes away.

Outside, the bell-tower unspools its carnival rendition
    of *Frère Jacques*, so I know it's either Sunday or noon.
        Grasshoppers fly up at every step
    like popping corn.
Everything is just a guess.

Look, the mounds of shiny mud have already paled:
    dirt giving itself to the prairie
        then riding west on the backs of whatever moves.

Crossing

I'm driving home, one eye on Iowa,
the fields golding in the lowering sun,
just past a sign warning *Don't Stop for Hitchhikers*
a small deer is poised at the edge of the road.
I consider stopping but there's no room,
the car packed tight with goods from the city.
There is nothing more for a mile or two,
then, gathered on the median
a herd of children sporting yellow jackets,
the stripes flaring in the headlights.
They look ready to run into oncoming traffic.
They'll never do it, I think, then swerve
a little in the new dark despite myself.

In the Field

Where cows graze
among mud and stones
and their own droppings
we spread our blanket
and sit close
for the first time
this whole week spent
in your mother's house,
we put our hands
on each other and slide
quiet under the enormous eyes
of cows, fogging up as I
spread my skirt (your mother said
a skirt for walking? yes I said
it's a walking skirt), and we
are moving together, the skirt
around us so the cows might wonder
but not the ruddy-faced man
bobbing suddenly over a hedge
or the one with him who
tipped his hat, later introduced
as your mother's favorite
neighbor at the market where
he shook your hand
a long time.

What if

one of what swam in (darling school daring the recesses)
managed to make its way a little farther this time, to stick around
and with a new found friend to hide among the flora
awhile, long enough, that is, to start becoming a resident,
to begin making a home, making this loaner space its own,
putting up gauzy curtains of webbing and some hoses,
all hooked up like the pneumatic tubes at the bank's drive-thru window,
whirring with a steady cycle of delivery and removal (so modern!):
necessity after necessity until nothing more is needed
or wanted and there's a knock at the door (not really a door, not really
a knock) and the lights flicker and the room shakes
and you realize it is you shaking the room, sounding the walls
for a way out or a way in, depending of course
on whether you look at this as an end or a beginning.

Stitch

The yard in summer is nettle and fruitless bramble: renters,
we don't bother much with landscape. All that poison
oak and ivy. And in the allergic tangle, nests. Don't dig
in this hard dirt with its sentries of prickles and biting gnats.
Behind a scrim of leggy weeds, a log of abandoned carpet,
weighted with weather and leaf fall. A groundhog dens there,
and the black cat that slinks and naps here mornings
suns there, preening a little under the frantic attention of blue jays.
I tried to lift it, the soggy roll, but it was already stitched
to earth. At best I might unravel it from the loose hem of root threads
enough to push it over. What sunless beetle scurries out, soft shell pale
as thumb flesh, what chiggers waiting to burrow in, what blind
and moley rodent-pups will wiggle, not yet foot-strong,
from the glare? Why do I want to go *in* there?

Peonies

Into the current, someone has thrown dozens of them,
densely petaled, red, fragrant, blooming
just now in yards all over town. Imagine a garden
growing up from the river, these blossoms atop tall stalks
surfacing from the gray water like crocuses do
in sudden bursts of color through the winter's loose mulch
in those first warm days.
                              Carp are birds, soaring
to the tops of long stems to sing into the flowers' centers—
they jump a little from the push of heads. A real-life
wide-winged bird swoops down at intervals, ascends and circles,
circles and drops again. The riverbank is movement,
shrubs shot through with small gray sparrows. The angler,
red shoulders underlined with precise white stripes, returns
to trill and trill. Some little insect life arrives
in swarms. This afternoon's loud duck shelters
in its own wing, beak tucked, the ducklings
hidden somewhere underneath.

4 am, Sitting in the Dark

And what I hear must be the cosmic wheel, time
lurching along at a hair and a tick, an all-directional stutter,

or an endless spin-your-partner dance, rotations
of velocity in momentary overlap. Why else

the streetlight's blink and flicker just as the hour's only car
glides by? Why else the birdsong suddenly stereophonic, then

suddenly silent but for one lone whistler, whistling?
Headlights read the ceiling's Braille and hush

(sound of a finger sealing a secret behind lips).
I recall the soccer field where I lay one night

to study stars— grass vibrant with cricket song,
mosquito buzz, workings of a thousand tiny jaws,

as I became increasingly still, a rock in rapids,
imperceptibly washing away.

Following You Up The Treehorn Trail

Tamaracks rise in a sharp line
above loose shale, the path feeding us
into a nest of wet cloud which slips
feathers down collars. The day is
blooming overhead like a movie set,
but I'm not watching this. Instead

I bruise the imprints of your steps
deep into the red clay. A welter
in the treetops drops a watery veil
between us, sheltering me with a blind swirl.
Your sudden stop a sharp surprise.
My guidebook warns of every hazard

but the cool curve of your neck. I'm quick
to turn away, wavering onto the shoulder,
the last season's ruined leaves
sliding under my feet. An unquiet whisper
insistent in my throat, a bold
croak leapfrogging *kiss, kiss.*

Echo

Throw your voice to the marsh and follow
its going: sky and sky's waving, watery clouds
at the knees of reeds, the leather of your shoes
darkening. Beneath farm dogs' yelps
and lowing, a conversation
of flank (fields rife with wind) rings
in shafts of hair, in grain elevators, rings
with the dull *yes* of metal where yesterday's eddies
fold in on themselves. Your call is falling
to pieces, floating into barley and cirrus, seeding
the horizon with riffs of spent breath.

Rabbit Farm

Los Alamos, New Mexico

As if a glance were a reach,
they flinch and twitch.
In each caged gaze
is a moon-sliver, splintering.

Fear is a live thing:
a ripple, rippling,
the record of a frog's leap
in widening circles.

Each hutch is lit
as though the sun reached in
instead of the red heat
of a small space.

Breath is a short leap, repeating.
Ears are skiffs of light,
feathery bows
leaning toward the least hope.

The Man in the Pyracantha

is so close he can feel the hot tips
of the thorns on his bare arm and the tops
of his linen-clad thighs. They catch
the threads, leave marks on his skin
like small red lips that have been kissing
too hard. The man in the pyracantha leans in
some, presses into the prickly limbs.
In the yard's lapping dark the bushes
are tall shadows and he needs to be inside
a shadow. In the streetlight
the cement walk glows white
and the grass is pale as dust and the flower beds
cast gray silhouettes that are too short
to conceal a standing man. The yellow window
drips light through half-open blinds
so here and there the leaves filter radiant tubes
spinning with moths, and June bugs
crash one after another into the window's screens
making more noise than the man who is after all
only breathing. The man
barely twitches even as blood surfaces
where his wrist is in barbs, and he suffers.
The front door swings open
to reveal a figure who is not the girl in the room—
not the flickers of skin, not the t-shirt that doesn't cover
the bare legs, not the girl who paces
and disappears for irritating seconds
then reappears with cherries or a clear glass
or the phone tucked on a shoulder or the cat.
The cat he sees now in the window, teeth bared
as if it can see through foliage with its strange eyes
on him. And the figure in the door

is in the yard now and now he must step out of the bush
and into the night and now he is laughing
with his heart loud as a shout in his chest
and he rushes toward the back where he knows
the streetlights won't reach and the neighbors' fences
are like a row of crooked teeth
whose dark gap he'll slip into
to be swallowed.

III.

Hatchery

The placemat in the restaurant has a picture:
a snake's fanged mouth open
for its tail. Not yet,
though everything is moving
with steady paces toward conclusion,
noticeably, as if racing.

In Minnesota the apple orchards are closing shop,
selling off the last jugs of cider. In Maine
the trees detonate their tops,
splatter the sky all month with scarlet.

Is it safe to say
whatever hasn't come to fruit is sterile?
The cherry tomato, for instance,
whose yellow flowers opened then fell to earth...

Here is that door from the *Late Late Show*,
its alarmingly slow opening, the inevitable entry—
perhaps a murderous humped creature dragging its lame leg, perhaps
a drenched stray tentatively wagging its bedraggled tail—
either way, the hinges reel an ominous dirge,
and there's no hurrying and no stopping
whatever will arrive.

Flash of Blue Catches
in a Corner of the Hippocampus

What the eye sees and does not want it winks inside
itself: encrypts in cortex. There are gaps
    where things slide through: rainy Thursday,
from a bus window a bent bird winging
open into a blue dome above a slickered crowd
and you are eight and lost: a rush of hems and strangers' backs,
jostle of boots, a damp stampede. Your world
    out of reach, neighborhood gone, friends, the low wall
behind the school, all gone in the seconds it took
to drop your hand and step away, look around, find yourself
    nowhere near knowing where you are—then the familiar
gloved grasp, still hurrying on. They would never know
how badly missing you had been.

Letter to John Berryman
After Jennifer Lynch

While you wrapped yourself into layers for your last winter walk, next door I may have been sitting on the blue carpet of my bedroom playing with china animals, inventing on a wooden checkerboard. While you made an anchor of despair, I may have been forming wet snow into a tight ball to toss at the side of your white house. I may have been whispering lullabies to your baby daughter, though I can't remember if she was born after or before. I remember ice-skating on Sundays with my family at the public rink. We went around the edges while in the middle my sister practiced spins and blade-led glides, her skirted form whirling among other spinners and other jumpers. I feared they would collide, those blades cocked at the ends of outstretched legs, though I don't think anyone ever did. Did you see the frosted branches bent and shining? Did the bridge funnel wind straight through your jacket to place a burning print on your chest? Did you lean into it then, as if into an embrace, pushing hard until you found yourself at the edge? I worry there's a small ice-seed that grows in the brain of someone I love; its eventual blossom smelling just like a bridge the moment a body steps from its rail.

Love Poem

Mark the tree of veins that arch and gather, send
their cargo straight to the stutterless heart

at near-perfect heat, unrelenting through night jolts
and dream chill, unstill even in the gesture of dressing

after professional speculation on the inner workings:
stethoscope to sternum, a solid set of curious fingers

that push and tap, sound out the glowing limbic limbs—
laser in for a look at the lookers—and no note of what drives

the whole careening overgrowth, some tiny seed
of bark-wrapped amber, its ambit of woven ectoplasm,

oh reasoning shell, unbearable murmur, thrum
of the cortextual flower: I blossom.

Nocturne

Remember the sea goats? Hollow-horned and randy,
nuzzling moss from jutting rocks, their

wet noses and white flecked matty pelts.
Ruminants at sun sets and rises, forelegs in the surf

to greet the tide. Twice in. Placid, unpanicked,
with no herder or heel-nipper near, they ride the waves.

Why make a story of pleasure? A salt lick. Twice
in the oranged water. Goat-gods, lives half in the cliffs

that rise up sharp where the sand ends. Their leap and scramble
traced by wakes of uprooted pebbles. Then into the cool swim

that mutes the bells and bleating to an echo,
the horns a chorus of glittering bugles, drifting in.

Hermit Crabs

Carting the hard weight
beyond reason, beyond
instinct's need to carry—
do they outgrow their shells
too slowly to notice
the pinch? Each scuttled step
a hobbled tussle
of mind under matter.
Or maybe the walls crack
with the ever-increasing
pressure. Time to move.
And you know this is taking it too far,
still, you wonder if one day
they notice they're suddenly lighter,
holding no notion
of what ever happened
to the old haunt.

City:

You're gorgeous in your fat bees and tulips. Your slim people in their spring blacks, unfurling glossy smirks. Leaves flock to branches like leaves. Pigeons too. Windows wave unwound bandages. I'm healing. No more pugs in sweaters, only slickers and plastic baggies in pale hues, and a fresh growth of fuzz on the undersides of everything. Damp fingers reach out of their exploded pods. Hulls and eggshells in unlikely cloisters. The racket must be incredible under there. Tennis courts bloom, moldering in flowery festival vines. Come hither. The world's replete with sudden knobbles, nodules, knees and pale elbows pacifying eyes. Flesh delights us, invites us. And fleas. Ribbed collars, woolen caps and gutter balls discovered clogging passageways at dances. The roof leaks, but we're on it, smoking. Even the neighbor's computer—hung out all winter in an undressed elm—now sports a new coat of fuchsia spray paint. Runners in squeaky trackers lurch past left over Easter lights. Lakes lap dance with puppies. Puppies are everywhere puppies could be. Then some fish surface, mouthy, an early crop, already ripe.

Postcard from Under the Weather

Where buildings with no balconies rise
from ungreen streets, jazzy with limpers,
leaners, strollers and sharp talk,
all thronging and shop-bagged and,
by noon, bedraggled (imagine
rain on red tile, an echo's echo), a bird
must have shaken last season's detritus
from a cluttered nest. Feather fall: it settled
on shoulders, was drawn under footsteps, it rode off
in hatbands and shirt cuffs. I captured
for your collection a single straw.
Home soon, love to all.

St. Theresa at the Apocalypse

Saint Theresa is deep undone, divided
to her marrow. A problem of faults
and bits. They've sawed her up good,
her sacred bone splinters and paper-thin
cross sections, her knuckles, scattered
to all of the altars that need her.
Her collectors—purveyors of the smallest parts,
receivers and protectors—must hinder
her safe return; all those vaults
and glassed-in cases. And if she wakes
to the trumpets' alarm
and tries to pull herself together, her once-dust
heart a magnet to draw the littlest bits
back home? One foot hopping across Rome
might meet in the Tiber a finger just in from Biloxi,
or Saint Peter of Ankles, hobbling through.
And if the pieces don't all show up on time,
what then? Who will guess the correct curve
of her holy knee, her left breast
perfect but for one white plaster nipple?

Nephography

Plain people...settle questions of weather for themselves...

A landscape of shining cotton, spectrum of pale brights: golden and cherry, salmon-streaked as sunrise. Snowcapped structures circling lakes—*there's one*—and in that valley a swath of chalky roofs, chimney smoke, the snaking veins of roads and streams and just there—*how like jumping beans they look!*—a balloon park. I am certain of the people—scattered in fields of radiant crops, delicate chilly fruit piling in baskets, stopping to shed their knit sweaters and pull hair off their necks into cloth caps, to scan for the storm that is always passing while their children chase at the field edges—certain they would let me stay, would refrain from eying my head of dark tangle or speculating on my gate of origin, respectful of my reluctance to sing in the fields. In the sweet air I will shed my black shoes with their punishing points, my tight dark tops, the computer-bag that digs ditches at shoulders. *Follow the path past the dairy,* they'll tell me, and I will. I'll ascend through white banks (I already know, each one is a prism waiting for release), trace the course into the thin air, winding up one lungful at a time, up to the steep top—to the height of mythic nests, hermits, the eagle's plunge—and watch for lightning to illuminate with flashes of dazzling relief.

Hopscotch

That barren game. A child on springs
making noise of a cement slab. We lost interest
in anything that didn't cause clamor or fire.
What we built was a cot of twigs, a gurney
to cradle a figure for melting. Soldiers barely wavered,
only smoked and blackened. Tiny pink baby dolls
boiled over from the inside. Their eyes tearing up
as if from bright lights. I never hurt an animal,
if you don't count the turtle kept in a locker—
I must have predicted a miraculous exit
like a hedgehog under the fence posts
where the carrots grow, or our neighbor's dog
in his nightly escape—at summer's end it was
(brittle crust with a swamp smell, the spiny pins of its legs
gone frothy) right where I left it, just lighter.

A Whole Summer Tumbles

itself onto the bed,
smothering me. An entire year.
Nearly a decade,
spooling out onto the covers,
heavy on my hot legs.
I can barely breathe
under the weight of fond memory.
My room refuses air
through ripped screens
that accommodate
insect wings, slivers of rain that shimmy
in the sheets. It was too much
to carry, those sweet drug-stung nights
that once stunned seasons
into passing. Such stickiness.
Like those flowers whose open mouths
are sugared with poison.
It is almost too much now
to consider the expanse—a phrase
my mother used—of wasted time:
though it was glorious.

Conveyance

It's always been summer on the roof, tarpaper and gravel, a door opening from steep steps at the end of the red-papered hall. Rob will bring an engine up one day when no one's around. Every week another piece: chassis then fenders, panels of various colors, a couple of bucket seats. We won't ask how he'll get it down. Every day we will climb, boys first to keep them from looking up shorts. On the roof we will strip off tops and recline on bright towels. The boys on their stomachs or sitting half turned, glancing and glancing over reddening shoulders. We'll empty our pockets for joints, a buck each, from the 7-11 clerk across the street. Once a day he'll step outside, light a cigarette, the sign. We'll never know about the car because Rob will go to South America for months, return with tire-sandals and no appetite, tan and pale at the same time. Riding his bike anywhere, he'll say he's against pollution, arrive always in a fog of sweat. We will move away or get married, buy cars or take trains across Europe; we will break our bones on ski lifts or on motorcycles, hurtling just ahead of our own wakes.

Fortune Cookie

Your luck depends on your kindness to others
and so you vow incessantly to smile. Smile

until you feel a mad thing creeping,
a rusted wheelbarrow screeching

eerie insults into the ear's dark cone. Examine
your left ventricle for the scroll tucked in

to its sink-hole, tight
as a spring; a gift. Finding it,

follow it, midriff to tartlet,
ankle scratch to lotto ticket, measuring

the pacing of pace. It'll eat
what you feed it, greedy gammon,

watching your fingers, greasing its lips;
not really wicked, just waiting, just wriggling

a little, just inching a finger, a lick
of a question, a loosening hook.

Metaphysics

Under the flowered cloth the table
has disappeared. You didn't notice? Ice shifted

a little in the drinks. You won't have thought
anything of the gesturing flame

in its candleless holder. You, who think the table
mustn't be where you left your blue glass:

there it is by the fern, buzzing
with gnats of golden light. A single petal

bowed like a small ship
has fallen into a spill, an ant somehow

its stranded passenger. The mobility of cutlery
is a flaw of your own mind, though not

in the way you imagine. There is something that pushes
everything, constantly. Explain, explain, explain.

Neither Sleeping nor Dreaming

Square-bodied spider tracing its tight loops
in silhouette, black against the glass glare—
sun angled so the gray sky flares
as if back-lit by flame—the web unseen.

Past the blazing gap the garden lingers,
this window my hundred sheep, the sleep gate
I swing wide while watching the sky fade.
From here the mind steps to the sill, leans out...

There are tall trees at the back of the yard,
birds high in their tall tops. A crow lowers
its beak to an apple, eyes sharp,
wind ruffling feathers and papery leaves.

Birds land or take flight and branches recoil
with small flurries, dropping fruit to the ground.
Where is the highest nest? Where is
that most delicate and elastic limb

to hold it? I stare at swaying treetops
until I feel myself in them, dizzy.
There are dreams like this. My body
pushing the boughs down, riding the long arc,

the uncontrollable swing—elated,
terrified, a little sick. Not what you
think, not sex, not only: I plunge
toward earth then ascend into sky, go too far.

I am a bird-woman, whistle and cage,
and I have chosen this precarious

station. At least in visions I
climb up in knowledge and fly down open.

And that I might crash disturbs me, and that
I might die occurs to me, and that I
will anyway is also true.
And my heart like a beating wing wakes me.

Printed in the United States
81712LV00004B/1-54